REAL
mvpkic

My Family Loves Me

Sophia Day®

Written by Megan Johnson   Illustrated by Stephanie Strouse

The Sophia Day® Creative Team-
Megan Johnson, Stephanie Strouse,
Kayla Pearson, Timothy Zowada, Mel Sauder

A **special thank you** to our team of reviewers who graciously
give us feedback, edits and help ensure that our products
remain accurate, applicable, and genuinely diverse.

Published and Distributed by MVP Kids Media, LLC -
Mesa, Arizona, USA
Printed by Prosperous Printing Inc. -
Shenzhen, China

Designed by Stephanie Strouse

ISBN 9781642552355
DOM Nov 2019,
Job # 11-007-01

May your childhood be filled with adventure, your days with hope and your learnings with wisdom, and may you continuously grow as an MVP Kid, preparing to lead a responsible, meaningful life.

- SOPHIA DAY

I know my family loves me

    when I'm woken with a smile.

My favorite way to start the day

    is snuggling for a while.

"More than all the colors in the sunrise that we view,

    I love you, my cuddle bug. I love you!"

What is the first
thing you do
when you wake up
in the morning?

I know my mommy loves me

when she guides me through the day,

helping me do all the things

I'll do myself someday.

"My love for you is bigger than

all the struggles you'll go through.

Ti amo, my little hero. I love you."
(tee ămo)

What are you learning to do for
yourself? What things do you
need help to do?
Ti amo is Italian for "I love you."

I know my parents love me

even when they have to leave.

I may miss them, but I know

they're working hard for our family.

Each time they remind me that they always come back, too!

"*Ich liebe dich*, my little princess. I love you!"
(esh lee-beh desh)

5

What kind of work
does your parent do?
Ich liebe dich is German
for "I love you."

I know my daddy loves me
when he comes home from a trip.
He shows me that he missed me
by bringing me a gift!

"Farther than around the world or way up to the moon,

我爱你, my greatest treasure. I love you!"
(wǒ ái ní)

What special gift has a family
member given to you?
我爱你 is Chinese
for "I love you."

8

I know my brother loves me

even when I'm mad or sad.

He helps me when I feel upset

and smiles when I'm glad.

"I'll brighten up your bad days, and share your good days, too.

אני אוהב אותך, little sis. I love you."

(ani ohev otach)

Who cheers you up when
you have a hard day?
אני אוהב אותך is Hebrew
for "I love you."

I know my sister loves me

    because she takes good care of me.

She wipes away each tear I cry

    and kisses my skinned knee.

"My love for you is tougher than any scrape or bruise.

    Я тебя люблю, brave warrior. I love you."

(yeah teh-byah loo-bloo)

Who makes you feel better when you are sick or hurt? **Я тебя люблю** is Russian for "I love you."

12

I know my family loves me,
and my brother and sister, too!
When our baby came along,
all of our love grew!

"Our arms and love are big enough to embrace all of you.

Nakupenda, little one. I love you!"

(nah-koo-PEND-ah)

How many people are in your family? *Nakupenda* is Swahili for "I love you."

What is your favorite thing
to play with your family?
Eu te amo is Portuguese
for "I love you."

I know my family loves me

  when we take some time to play.

When Uncle is the goalie

  he lets a few balls get away.

"Every day, all the time, forever, win or lose,

  Eu te amo, shining star. I love you!"

(ee-oh tee ah-moh)

I know my auntie loves me

when she saves me the last cookie.

I know she thinks about me

when she's making special goodies.

"You're sweeter to me than any treat or candy chew.
أحبكِ, my little sugar. I love you!"

(oo-HEH-boo-kee)

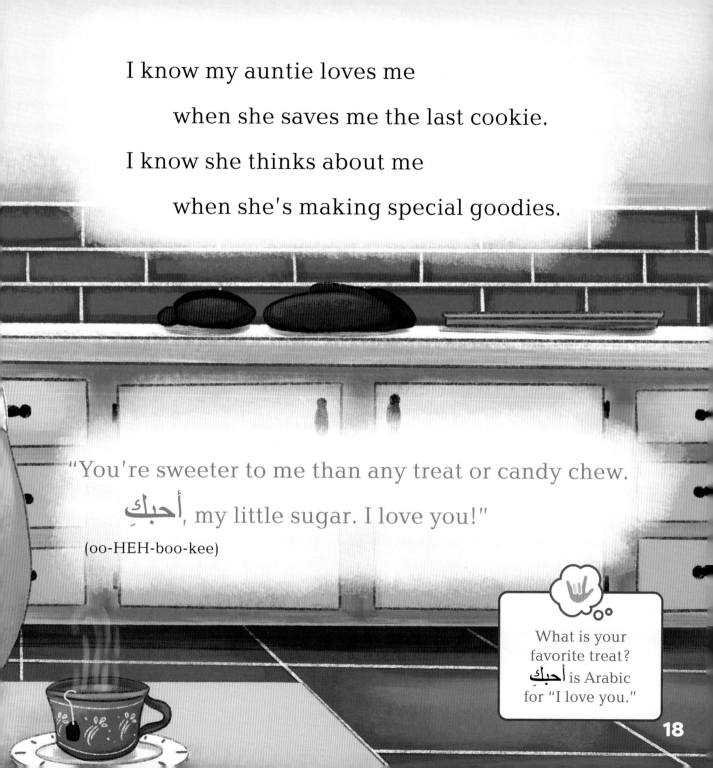

What is your
favorite treat?
أحبكِ is Arabic
for "I love you."

18

I know my parents love me
  because they give me all I need:
a home, good food and family,
  clothes, toys, and books to read.

"All that I could ever want, I already have in you!

मैं तुमसे प्यार करता हूँ, my darling. I love you."

(may thoom-se pyar kar-tha hoom)

What things do we need to live? मैं तुमसे प्यार करता हूँ is Hindi for "I love you."

20

I know my grandpa loves me when

he fills us all with laughter.

Telling jokes and tickling,

it's hard to settle after!

"Stronger than a superhero, my love for you is true.

사랑해, my tumbly buddy. I love you!"

(sah-rang-hey)

Who makes
you laugh?
사랑해 is Korean
for "I love you."

21

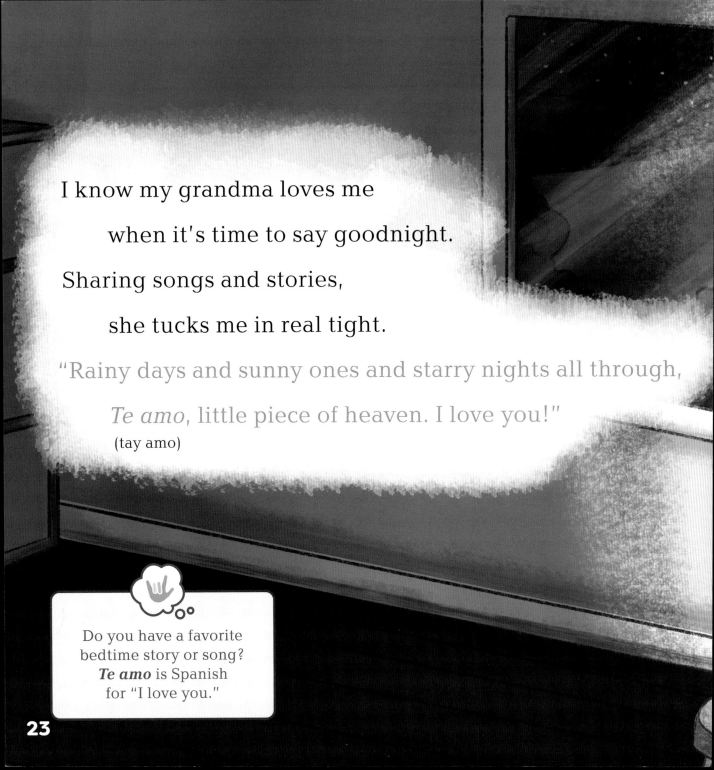

I know my grandma loves me

when it's time to say goodnight.

Sharing songs and stories,

she tucks me in real tight.

"Rainy days and sunny ones and starry nights all through,

Te amo, little piece of heaven. I love you!"
(tay amo)

Do you have a favorite
bedtime story or song?
Te amo is Spanish
for "I love you."

I know that you love me

    when you read a book with me.

"Spending time with you, my love,

    is where I want to be.

Of all the treasures in the world, it's you I'll always choose!

    I'm so glad you're in my family. I love you!"

How do you like to spend time with your family?

meet our

mvpkids

featured in
My Family Loves Me™

Olivia Wagner

Lucas Miller

LeBron Miller

Liam Johnson

Frankie Russo

Leo Russo

Julia Rojas

Yong Chen

Faith Jordan

Ezekiel Jordan

Sarah Cohen-Goldstein

Aanya Patel

Gabby González

Miriam Nasser

Annie James

Blake James

HELPFUL TEACHING TIPS

Head. Heart. Hand.

Informing Minds

Families of all types can raise healthy children. Single parents, married partners, blended families, adoptive, and foster families and families in any socio-economic situation all look different but can all be successful. On your most challenging days, remember that as long as you're doing your best to connect with your child and provide a safe and loving environment, you're succeeding!

Evidence shows that engaging play between children and their parents aides in healthy brain development and supports math and reading success. Engaging play may include literacy activities such as reading books and pointing to the pictures, playing games, doing puzzles, building with blocks, and even discussions about the day's events can encourage problem solving skills.

It's never too late to be intentional about building a healthy bond with your child. When a caregiver responds quickly to a child's need, pathways for trust are developed. Similarly, eye contact between parent and child releases the hormone oxytocin, a pleasure chemical, which deepens bonds and calms a child. The more frequently the brain's pathways are reinforced, the more quickly these calming hormones are produced in the future, influencing a child's overall body chemistry and disposition.

Moving Hearts

Parents who give positive and predictable attention to their children help them learn to manage their behavior and emotions. Children need to know their world is a safe and reliable place where they can express their needs and expect predictable and loving responses.

A strong attachment to a parent figure is one of the greatest factors in a child's social and emotional success in later life. Healthy attachment is believed to reduce the likelihood of later addictions and other risky behaviors.

A heart of obedience is gained by a child's bond with the caregiver. A child is more motivated to behave out of love and respect rather than fear. The obedience motivated by a desire to please the parent is full obedience from the heart. Obedience driven by fear of punishment is often only outward while the child inwardly grows angry and more rebellious.

It is natural for children to wonder whether mom or dad still love them when they act out. The first step in correction should be to connect with your child on an emotional level and assure your child of your unwavering love. This will not only reassure your child, but will also help calm you to be able to discipline in an appropriate manner without anger.

Moving Hearts

While frustrating for parents, separation anxiety is natural and a good indicator of a healthy bond between parent and child. Do not shame your child for feeling anxious about separation. IInstead, reassure your child of your love and that you will return. Ask the caregiver to engage your child in his or her favorite activity to help ease the transition, but do not try to trick your child and risk losing his trust.

Develop loving rituals with your child for different parts of the day: a daily story time with cuddles, a special way to wake up, serving a favorite meal, a favorite song to sing at bedtime or a secret handshake are some examples of ways you can create memories that form a unique bond between you and your child.

Try creating family memory books. Place pictures of your children and family around your home. Traditions, family creeds, celebrations, and family meetings are some ways to build your family culture and sense of belonging for your child.

Parenting is difficult. If you find yourself in a challenging season with your child, find a support group or another parent who can offer some wisdom. Contact a local religious body, a family counselor, or social media groups. Especially if your child has medical needs or a disability, was adopted or has suffered other trauma, there are many great resources you may find through therapists, online support groups, children's hospitals, and other community organizations. Take care of yourself and take breaks when you need to so you can give your best to your child.

Directing Hands

For additional tip and reference information, visit **www.mvpkids.com**.

Grow up with our MVP Kids

CELEBRATE!™
Board Books
Ages 0-6

Our **CELEBRATE!™** board books for toddlers and preschoolers focus on social, emotional, educational and physical needs. Helpful Teaching Tips are included in each book to equip parents to guide their children deeper into the subject of each book.

MIGHTY TOKENS
READ TOGETHER
Ages 4-8

Our **Mighty Tokens™** paperback books for Pre-K to Grade 3 help emerging readers experience positive concepts with their parents. Children will learn valuable reading skills as their parents read one side of the page and your child is encouraged to read the other side.

help me BECOME
Early Elementary
Ages 4-10

Our **Help Me Become™** series for early elementary readers tells three short stories of our MVP Kids® inspiring character growth. Each story concludes with a discussion guide to help your child process the story and apply the concepts.

help me UNDERSTAND™
Elementary
Ages 6-12

Our **Help Me Understand™** series for elementary readers shares the stories of our MVP Kids® learning to understand and manage a specific emotion. Readers will gain tools to take responsibility for their own emotions and develop healthy relationships.

Celebrate! Paperbacks

Ages 4-8

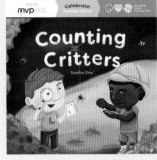
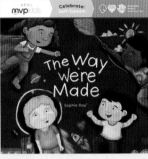

Our **Celebrate!™** paperback books for Pre-K to Grade 2 focus on social and emotional learning. Helpful Teaching Tips are included to equip mentors and parents. These books are perfect for classrooms and home schooling!

Inspire Me-Books™

Our interactive **Inspire Me-Book™** apps are designed to expand the experience of our content. Functions include audio of Sophia Day reading the book, learn-to-read options, and interactive games.

www.mvpkidsED.com

DON'T MISS OUT!
Social Emotional Learning (SEL)
Curriculum for Early Learners
• *Entire year's worth of SEL lesson plans*
• *8 MVP Kids puppets*
• *Audio tracks and many more resources to build a classroom full of MVP Kids!*

www.mvpkids.com